A FRUITFUL LIFE *of* Significance

NINE WORDS THAT CAN CHANGE YOUR LIFE
AND THE LIVES OF PEOPLE AROUND YOU!

JEFFREY L. HORNER

Endorsements

I've known Jeffrey for over 23 years, and in that time, I've seen his commitment to God and his genuine desire to help others become their best. Sharing from his life's journey, Jeffrey will challenge you to experience A Fruitful Life of Significance. He doesn't just speak about the power beyond praying these nine words, but it is obvious to see them in operation in his own life. This book will add strength and encouragement to you and those around you!

Mike Haman
Lead Pastor of Healing Place Church

The best thing about *A Fruitful Life of Significance* is that its author, my friend Jeffrey Horner, is the real deal. He is a true practitioner of everything you'll read in these pages. Every word comes directly from his heart! This book can bless you and bless others through you. Get ready to experience a straightforward, easy read; 100% authentic, 0% fluff!

Chuck Bush
Filmmaker/Author

Knowing Jeffrey for almost five years has been such a Blessing. His walk with our Lord and Savior Jesus coupled with a "let's be real" attitude, make him a Warrior Disciple for the Kingdom. God has used him in a mighty way to encourage me in my walk with the Lord, and I know *"A Fruitful Life of Significance"* will do the same for you and those you share it with. 1Thessalonians 5:11 *"Therefore encourage one another and build each other up as you are already doing."* HCSB

Bax Kegans
Gulf South Men

Jeffrey has been a friend for almost 30 years. I'm excited about what God is doing in and through him. Jeffrey loves God and cares deeply about pleasing Him for God's Glory. Jeffrey peels back the veneer and becomes vulnerable as he seeks the face of God. I highly recommend that you read this book. You'll see God transforming Jeffrey more into His image each day. Jeffrey invites all of us to come along to take part in God's transformation.

M.L. Woodruff
Minister of Sports Outreach
Istrouma Baptist Church

Dedication

I dedicate this book to all the people who've prayed for me, studied with me, or guided me through difficult times in my life!

I also dedicate this book to my loving wife, Aimee, who's always been my rock, especially when I struggled to believe that God would provide. Her unwavering faith in God reassured me and let me know that all would be fine. I love you, Aimee.

Most of all, I dedicate this book to Jesus, who has never abandoned me. I have no doubt he'll continue to walk with me until I see him in heaven!

Forward

This book by my great friend Jeffrey Horner is truly going to be a significant blessing to everyone that reads it. He and I became friends years ago at our weekly businessmen's luncheon here at Bethany Church. Jeffrey became one of our table leaders and has been a very close friend and brother in Christ since the first day I met him. We still help each other lead a group of men weekly for a bible study, and at the close of our meeting, we pray over each other's needs. In one of our meetings, I had the opportunity to share the "seven" things I pray over my family and friends daily. They're Wisdom, Purpose, Protection, Purity, Peace, Prosperity, and Blessings. Well, in this awesome book, Brother Jeffrey expounds upon these seven words by adding, Overflow, and Favor. So, in reading "A Fruitful Life of Significance" Brother Jeffrey points out how praying these "nine" powerful words over himself, his family, his friends, and businesses can make us all have a God-fearing, loving, and caring heart for the Lord. To have a Significant Life on Earth, we must all do what God has called us to do. Brother Jeffrey testifies to us how that can be achieved for God's glory. As you read this book be prepared to have your heart, mind, and soul ready to be blessed, so you can be a blessing. As Brother Jeffrey always closes out our time together with these powerful words, "I love you, Brother!" I love you too, Brother Jeffrey. Again, I highly recommend that we all purchase and read "A Fruitful Life of Significance," so we can all move toward the amazing life God has for us all.

Hank Henagan
Associate Pastor
Bethany Church

Jeffrey L Horner

Table of Contents

Wisdom

"IF ANY OF YOU LACKS WISDOM, YOU SHOULD ASK GOD, WHO GIVES GENEROUSLY TO ALL WITHOUT FINDING FAULT, AND IT WILL BE GIVEN TO YOU."

JAMES 1:5

Purpose

30 "LOVE THE LORD YOUR GOD WITH ALL YOUR HEART AND WITH ALL YOUR SOUL AND WITH ALL YOUR MIND AND WITH ALL YOUR STRENGTH. 31 THE SECOND IS THIS: 'LOVE YOUR NEIGHBOR AS YOURSELF.' THERE IS NO COMMANDMENT GREATER THAN THESE."

MARK 12:30-31

Protection

¹"WHOEVER DWELLS IN THE SHELTER OF THE MOST HIGH WILL REST IN THE SHADOW OF THE ALMIGHTY. ²I WILL SAY OF THE LORD, 'HE IS MY REFUGE AND MY FORTRESS, MY GOD, IN WHOM I TRUST.'"

PSALMS 91:1-2

Purity

*"FINALLY, BROTHERS AND SISTERS, WHATEVER IS TRUE, WHATEVER IS NOBLE, WHATEVER IS RIGHT, WHATEVER IS **PURE**, WHATEVER IS LOVELY, WHATEVER IS ADMIRABLE — IF ANYTHING IS EXCELLENT OR PRAISEWORTHY — THINK ABOUT SUCH THINGS."*

PHILIPPIANS 4:8

Peace

⁶"DO NOT BE ANXIOUS ABOUT ANYTHING, BUT IN EVERY SITUATION, BY PRAYER AND PETITION, WITH THANKSGIVING, PRESENT YOUR REQUESTS TO GOD. ⁷AND THE PEACE OF GOD, WHICH TRANSCENDS ALL UNDERSTANDING, WILL GUARD YOUR HEARTS AND YOUR MINDS IN CHRIST JESUS."

PHILIPPIANS 4:6-7

Prosperity
*"IN HIS DAYS MAY THE RIGHTEOUS FLOURISH AND **PROSPERITY** ABOUND TILL THE MOON IS NO MORE."*

PSALM 72:7

Blessings
[24] "THE LORD BLESS YOU AND KEEP YOU; [25] THE LORD MAKE HIS FACE SHINE ON YOU AND BE GRACIOUS TO YOU; [26] THE LORD TURN HIS FACE TOWARD YOU AND GIVE YOU PEACE."

NUMBERS 6:24-26

Favor
"SURELY, LORD, YOU BLESS THE RIGHTEOUS; YOU SURROUND THEM WITH YOUR FAVOR AS WITH A SHIELD."

PSALM 5:12

Overflow
[5] "YOU PREPARE A TABLE BEFORE ME IN THE PRESENCE OF MY ENEMIES. YOU ANOINT MY HEAD WITH OIL; MY CUP OVERFLOWS. [6] SURELY YOUR GOODNESS AND LOVE WILL FOLLOW ME ALL THE DAYS OF MY LIFE, AND I WILL DWELL IN THE HOUSE OF THE LORD FOREVER."

PSALM 23:5-6

Author's note

Most of us want to be able to help our spouse, our family, or our close friends in any way we can, but sometimes we just don't know how to go about it. It can be frustrating to not know what to do, at the least that's how it used to be for me. That is until a friend of mine, a great spiritual brother, Hank Henagan, shared with me his method of praying for others. He explained that during his study time every morning, he prayed seven words over each of his family members, and others, asking God to bless them in those specific areas. I tried it, loved it, and then added two more words to the list!

- Wisdom

- Purpose

- Protection

- Purity

- Peace

- Prosperity

- Blessings

- Favor

- Overflow

Praying this way has been a game-changer, or I should say a life-changer for me. God has blessed me with such joy and peace. He's relieved me of the helplessness and frustration I felt when I didn't know how to help a loved one. Now I'm confident I'm lifting them up to our Almighty God, who DOES know their needs and can help them. Brother Hank also revealed to me that by practicing this prayer technique for others, I'm serving them in a way that contributes the best help I could ever offer anyone.

I hope this book will encourage you to serve those around you by praying for them, whether it's one of these words or all nine of them. Watch how God blesses and impacts both the person that's being prayed for, and you, the pray-er, with a fruitful and significant life!

Chapter 1

Wisdom

Scripture

"If any of you lacks wisdom, you should ask God, who gives generously to all without finding fault, and it will be given to you."

James 1:5

[13] *"Blessed are those who find wisdom, those who gain understanding,* [14] *for she is more profitable than silver, and her wages are better than gold."*

Proverbs 3:13-14

Dictionary

Wisdom is the soundness of an action or decision with regard to the application of experience, knowledge, and good judgment.

How does a person get wisdom? According to the dictionary and most people in the world, a person gains wisdom with age, experience, and knowledge. The Bible says wisdom comes from God. So, if you or a loved one is in need of wisdom, and you don't have the time or don't want to wait for age, experience, or knowledge to kick in, go to the source!

"If any of you lacks wisdom, you should ask God, who gives generously to all without finding fault, and it will be given to you."

James 1:5

I became a Christian at the age of twenty-three. When I read James 1:5, I thought that when I'd ask God for wisdom, He'd tell me what He wanted me to do or where He wanted me to go as soon as I asked. It took me a few years, but I finally realized for me to hear God communicating with me, I had to learn how to listen for the voice of the Holy Spirit from within me.

"The person without the Spirit does not accept the things that come from the Spirit of God but considers them foolishness, and cannot understand

THEM BECAUSE THEY ARE DISCERNED ONLY
THROUGH *THE SPIRIT."*

1 CORINTHIANS 2:14
(EMPHASIS IS MINE)

The key was to differentiate the Holy Spirit's voice from all others. For the first twenty-three years of my life, the voices that had an impact on me had influenced me in ways that weren't Godly.

I distinctly remember a specific situation that I experienced when I began to learn to recognize the Holy Spirit's voice. I was standing in a line at a local pharmacy behind an older lady who was struggling to pay for her prescription. My heart and my soul were saying "help her," which I believed was the Holy Spirit prompting me. But in my mind, I heard one of those old worldly voices telling me, "You can't do that. It's going to embarrass her, and besides, you don't have the money right now." Sadly, I gave in to the old voice, and I felt horrible for making that decision for hours. Later that day, I shared the incident with my wife and told her how sad I felt about it. She told me that when the Holy Spirit taps me on my shoulder and tells me to do something, I should do it. She said never to let money or anything else control me or stand in the way of obeying God's voice. That was a turning point in my life. From then on, I started listening to that voice and acting on it.

For me to learn to discern the Holy Spirit's voice, I had to train my spirit to be still and quiet. Once I learned how to block out all of the noise from the world, I was then able to hear the wisdom of God through the Holy Spirit.

Unfortunately, being still and quiet is not my spirit's typical state. I'm sure many other people are the same. When I need wisdom, I have to get myself quiet and be still as the first part of Psalm 46:10 directs.

> *HE SAYS, "BE STILL AND KNOW THAT I AM GOD."*
>
> *PSALM 46:10A*

I block out all the noise that's around me, and I get into the moment. My consciousness is kept clear of thoughts of tomorrow, next week, or the future. I open my mind and my heart for God to talk to me and to guide me through whatever difficult decision or situation I face.

When you ask God to bless your loved ones with wisdom, either generally or for a specific situation, go a step further and ask Him to help them learn how to be still and quiet and to give them discernment in learning to listen to the Holy Spirit's voice. I believe that God also gives us wisdom by speaking to us through scriptures. It took me the longest time to apply God's word to my life and to allow Him to help me deal with any issues that arose. I've always believed that the Bible is true and that it's the Word of God; I haven't always believed that it was practical for my life. I learned that while searching for guidance, the Holy Spirit would lay verses I had read and learned in the past on my heart. They encouraged me, and I found them helpful where I needed guidance. There have been other times while reviewing passages or verses of the scriptures that I've read many times before, that the Holy Spirit has revealed something new and fresh to me.

Another suggestion when praying for wisdom for your loved one would be to ask God to speak to them through His scriptures. Even if the person you're praying for doesn't habitually, or even ever read the Bible, God can still put scriptures into their ears and minds in other ways that will allow them to gain the insight and wisdom they need. Don't limit God on what He can do. You just pray and ask; let Him work out the how.

In a devotional that I read at OurDailyBread. com, Amy Peterson wrote, "To seek wisdom is ultimately to seek God, the source of all wisdom and understanding. And the wisdom that comes from above is worth more than any treasure we could ever imagine."[†] If you believe what Ms. Peterson wrote, then when you pray for God to bless your loved ones and friends with wisdom, you are also praying for their spiritual growth.

Pray for the Holy Spirit to guide them every day and to draw them closer to the Lord. What a powerful and dynamic gift to give someone! **Get Wisdom!**

Chapter 2

Purpose

Scripture

^{30} *"LOVE THE LORD YOUR GOD WITH ALL YOUR HEART AND WITH ALL YOUR SOUL AND WITH ALL YOUR MIND AND WITH ALL YOUR STRENGTH. ^{31}THE SECOND IS THIS: 'LOVE YOUR NEIGHBOR AS YOURSELF.' THERE IS NO COMMANDMENT GREATER THAN THESE."*

MARK 12:30-31

Dictionary

Purpose is the reason for which something is done or created or for which something exists.

January 20th of 1984 was a turning point in my life. It was that day, in a small church in southern Baton Rouge, Louisiana, where I turned my life over to Jesus. I've spent many years studying, trying to figure out my journey and purpose. For nine years, I led many Bible studies. I was heavily involved in prison ministry, where I led both worship and Bible studies. Yet I still struggled with sin and felt unable to please God.

I thought I could lose my salvation and felt I always had to work to keep it. It wasn't until I left that church did I realize I was saved by His grace – I couldn't lose my salvation, and I didn't have to work for it. I finally understood the love that Jesus Christ and God really had for me. That's when I was released from works, shame, and guilt. I started doing the work for God because of what He did for me, not for what I could do for Him. My salvation was intact. I wanted to work for Him because of His love for me, not because I feared He'd take His love away from me or because I'd lose my salvation. God's message is clear.

[8] *"FOR IT IS BY GRACE YOU HAVE BEEN SAVED, THROUGH FAITH – AND THIS IS NOT*

FROM YOURSELVES, IT IS THE GIFT OF GOD — [9] NOT BY WORKS, SO THAT NO ONE CAN BOAST."

EPHESIANS 2:8-9

"NEVER WILL I LEAVE YOU; NEVER WILL I FORSAKE YOU."

HEBREWS 13:5A

He would always be with me, no matter what I did. We should serve Him because of love, not out of obligation. My journey and purpose were more about grace and mercy. I realized that I could never work or be good enough to keep my salvation. Past experiences or some religion surely has many of you trying to figure out what your purpose is and how you're going to please God.

Works and shame tell you that you could lose your salvation. I'm here to let you know that there's no condemnation in those that are in Christ Jesus.

"THEREFORE, THERE IS NOW NO CONDEMNATION FOR THOSE WHO ARE IN CHRIST JESUS..."

ROMANS 8:1

No matter what you do, God is always there. If you're battling with sin in your life, remember God is there to help you through the struggle.

"NO TEMPTATION HAS OVERTAKEN YOU EXCEPT WHAT IS COMMON TO MANKIND. AND GOD IS FAITHFUL; HE WILL NOT LET YOU BE TEMPTED BEYOND WHAT YOU CAN BEAR. BUT WHEN YOU ARE TEMPTED, HE WILL ALSO PROVIDE A WAY OUT SO THAT YOU CAN ENDURE IT."

1 CORINTHIANS 10:13

Remember that God helps us with our temptation from sin. When we do sin and repent, he'll help us through it.

Repent: Someone who repents changes his inner self - his old way of thinking, lives his life in a way that proves repentance; and seeks God's purpose for his life.

God forgives us our sins. However, there are consequences when we sin, even if we've repented. I had someone tell me a story about when their daughter was involved in a car wreck where she was at fault.

The person she hit said, "Honey, it's alright as long as we're not hurt; our cars can be fixed."

To me, that is Mercy. There are still consequences, though. The cars had to be repaired. It was the daughter's fault, so she and her insurance company had to take care of it.

Now, if the person had said, "I'll take care of my car and yours," that would have been Grace. Do you hear that? God not only forgives us of our sin; He also forgets and will continue to bless us.

What does that have to do with our purpose? We need to be the person who shows grace and mercy to the people that hurt us or mistreat us, even if it conflicts with every part of our being. That's why our purpose HAS to be going to the higher ground.

> *[14]"You are the light of the world. A town built on a hill cannot be hidden. [15]Neither do people light a lamp and put it under a bowl. Instead they put it on its stand, and it gives light to everyone in the house. [16]In the same way, let your light shine before others, that they may see your good deeds and glorify your Father in heaven."*
>
> *Matthew 5:14-16*

God wants to help you with the little things, the big things, and everything in between.

> *"In the same way, the Spirit helps us in our weakness. We do not know what we ought to pray for, but the Spirit*

HIMSELF INTERCEDES FOR US THROUGH WORDLESS GROANS."

ROMANS 8:26

Even when you don't know what to say, the Holy Spirit groans to the Father to be able to help you be the man or woman that He wants you to be.

"AND MY GOD WILL MEET ALL YOUR NEEDS ACCORDING TO THE RICHES OF HIS GLORY IN CHRIST JESUS."

PHILIPPIANS 4:19

Once I realized that my needs would always be taken care of, I was able to get out of myself and help and serve those around me. I could talk to men that were struggling with addictions or their walk and their journey. I understood what my purpose was. When I pray for purpose over someone, it helps me remember what my purpose is on this earth.

I want you to do something whenever someone comes to your mind. Pray for them. Stop where you are, stop what you're doing, think about this person, and pray for them. It might be just a simple, "God, comfort them in whatever they're going through," or "Oh Lord, you know what their need is right now. Help them in whatever is going on with them." You'll be amazed at how that helps you and your relationship with God. I've put this into practice, and it's been a blessing for my connection with Him. While this act was foreign to me at first, I remembered to do it when someone came to my mind, and it became a habit.

Great people I've looked up to my whole adult life have repeatedly told me I'm here for a reason. While I've always agreed with them, I've never understood what that reason was until I got older. They got me to start thinking about what my purpose is; today, it's completely different from what it was when I was growing up.

When I was a child, I understood my purpose was to obey my mother. I had no clue there was another purpose for me being on this earth, other than that. I just did what I was told. My mom did the best that she could in spite of her circumstances. Almost all of us have had parents or mentors that nurtured us as we were growing up. I am, as a lot of you are, from a broken, dysfunctional home. When I was eight years old, my mother took my nine-month-old sister and me on a long, hot train ride. I didn't understand at the time that my mom had left my dad. From then on, she had to raise my sister and me on her own, with some help of her parents. My purpose at the tender age of eight changed – I had to become the man of the house. Not that anyone taught me what that meant, at eight; it just happened. My mom lost all of her friends and her husband and had to move seven hundred and twenty miles away to live with her parents. We were broke and broken. My sister and I became *her* purpose.

That said, we all have a purpose. How do we approach it? Will we let circumstances dictate our purpose, or will we be proactive?

My mom got a job. She did all she could to protect and feed us. Because she had to care for us, she was thrown into having to be proactive. She did the best she knew how, no matter how hard she found it. She just did it.

Are we letting circumstances dictate our purpose, or are we purposeful with our walk on this earth?

It wasn't until my fifties that I truly understood what it meant to have a purpose in my life. My purpose before that was money and how to stay ahead of all my bills. Sure, I was a Christian who thought I depended on God. I relied upon

Him off and on, although I would take back control. That is until I'd realize that that wasn't working. When that would happen, I'd repent and get back on track, still not fully aware of my real purpose in life. I provided for my family – actually, God provided for us – and we never lacked for anything we needed, ever.

> *"THE LORD IS MY SHEPHERD, I LACK NOTHING."*
> *PSALM 23:1 – A PSALM OF DAVID*

One day, as I struggled with a question that I've dealt with often – "Why am I here?" – a voice came to me when I read the following scripture:

> [30] *"LOVE THE LORD YOUR GOD WITH ALL YOUR HEART AND WITH ALL YOUR SOUL AND WITH ALL YOUR MIND AND WITH ALL YOUR STRENGTH.* [31] *THE SECOND IS THIS: LOVE YOUR NEIGHBOR AS YOURSELF. THERE IS NO COMMANDMENT GREATER THAN THESE."*
> *MARK 12:30-31*

When I found out that a spiritual brother of mine was praying *purpose* over his family and friends – praying for them without them knowing – I knew that Mark 12:30-31 *was* my purpose. I had to love God with ALL of my heart and love my neighbor, too.

What did that mean? I needed to get out of my comfort zone and think of others, no matter who they were. That meant anyone, from the person that cut me off in traffic, to people in the checkout line at the grocery store. Maybe the cashier is having a bad day because so many people don't take the time to be nice to them. The next time you're in the checkout line, I'd like you to look at the cashier and speak to him or her. With inflection in your voice, say, "HELLO, how are you doing today?"

After you pick her or him off the floor, be aware of their response. Usually, you'll see them filled with joy and happiness because you've engaged them and appreciated them. Look them in the eye and let them know you care. You might have had a bad day, but I tell you what, it will fill your heart more than theirs. I promise!

It may be scary at first, but it gets easier and more fulfilling over time. I remember a particular occasion when I got into an elevator with a bunch of people who neither looked at each other nor said a word. I decided that the next time I stepped into an elevator that I would push myself out of my comfort zone and say, in my southern accent, "HEY! How are y'all today?"

The first chance I got, I did it. When I got off the elevator, everyone was laughing and in a better mood! Why? Because I got out of myself and encouraged them. When I go down the Piccadilly Cafeteria line, I talk with all the people serving my food. I always get more food than everyone else! I definitely don't engage them for that reason, and I don't need it, but when you acknowledge others with a joyful heart and a skip in your step, great things happen to you. The same goes for those who receive your kind interaction.

Elisa Morgan said, "God stitches His love and purposes in our hearts that we might experience Him for ourselves and demonstrate His handiwork to others."††

When you pray purpose over someone's life, believe that God will reveal their purpose to them and that they'll put it into practice. It'll bless you just as it does them. What's your **Purpose?**

Chapter 3

Protection

Scripture

[1] "Whoever dwells in the shelter of the Most High will rest in the shadow of the Almighty. [2]I will say of the Lord, 'He is my refuge and my fortress, my God, in whom I trust.'"

Psalms 91:1-2

Dictionary

Protection is a person or thing that prevents someone or something from suffering harm or injury.

As I start this chapter, I can't help but think about what protection means for my family. I erected a fence surrounding my property, including a gate that blocks my driveway. It, along with a security system, protects us from anyone who tries to get in without permission. I carry personal protection to use to defend myself or my family, whether we're in our car or away from home. It's with confidence that I say I can protect the ones I love. After all of the time and effort that it took to plan and make all of these things part of our reality, I have to wonder if I'm the one that's genuinely protecting my family. Is there something greater than myself taking care of us, not just physically, but spiritually, emotionally, and mentally?

I must ask myself, "Am I absolutely protected?" If someone truly wants to hurt me or someone I care for or love, can I really protect us? As a man, I feel I've been blessed with the wisdom to think ahead and be proactive. I don't act like there's a monster around every corner, nor do I wear rose color glasses. There are dangers in the world, and I know it. God certainly wants us to be smart when we walk through life. He wants us to protect ourselves and others from evil.

When I watch a television show, I always think it's unfortunate when a young girl walking by herself chooses to save time by taking a short cut through a dark alley. Inside, I yell at the screen, "What are you thinking?" It usually doesn't end well for her. We have brains, and we need to use them. Still, we don't need to live our lives in fear; that isn't healthy for any of us.

We should have respect for the evil that's out there.

> *"BE ALERT AND OF SOBER MIND. YOUR ENEMY THE DEVIL PROWLS AROUND LIKE A ROARING LION LOOKING FOR SOMEONE TO DEVOUR."*
>
> *1 PETER 5:8*

How do we not let fear run our lives? The easy answer is through faith.

I say the easy answer is faith, but why is it so hard for us to believe that there's a God that's great enough to protect us? One reason might be you don't believe we're worth being protected. Maybe we've done something horrible in our lives. Many people don't believe they deserve a safe life or one where peace and joy surrounds them. Have you done something bad to hurt someone? Are you concerned that you could never be forgiven, and have someone or something protect you? Are you completely broken? Keep reading. I might have an answer that could help you heal your brokenness.

Another reason some people feel this way is because we believe we can take care of ourselves. Maybe you think, "I have a ten-foot-tall fence and I carry a gun legally. I've got this!"

There's also the mindset that bad things happen to other people. You may think, "That would never happen to me." When it dawned on me that the protection I needed was not physical, but spiritual, my life was changed. I realized that there was a war going on around me that was not visible to my eyes. That epiphany changed my thinking.

"FOR OUR STRUGGLE IS NOT AGAINST FLESH AND BLOOD, BUT AGAINST THE RULERS, AGAINST THE AUTHORITIES, AGAINST THE POWERS OF THIS DARK WORLD AND AGAINST THE SPIRITUAL FORCES OF EVIL IN THE HEAVENLY REALMS."

EPHESIANS 6:12

The reality is that there truly is a war going on around us and negative things are going to happen to us and our loved ones. This awareness made me wonder how could I be protected and how I could shield my family and the people around me. When I understood that the fight was a spiritual one, I knew the answers were in the scriptures. I studied what I needed to be ready to do battle when it came to my doorstep.

We can fight and protect ourselves and our families. If you haven't done it yet, turn your life over to God. Surrender to the saving Grace of Jesus Christ. I plead with you to do so now. Your life and eternal life depend on your decision.

Let's continue and armor up.

[10] "FINALLY, BE STRONG IN THE LORD AND IN HIS MIGHTY POWER. [11]PUT ON THE FULL ARMOR OF GOD, SO THAT YOU CAN TAKE YOUR STAND AGAINST THE DEVIL'S SCHEMES. [12]FOR OUR STRUGGLE IS NOT AGAINST FLESH AND BLOOD, BUT AGAINST THE RULERS, AGAINST THE AUTHORITIES, AGAINST THE POWERS OF THIS DARK WORLD AND AGAINST THE SPIRITUAL FORCES OF EVIL IN THE HEAVENLY REALMS. [13]THEREFORE PUT ON THE FULL ARMOR OF GOD, SO THAT WHEN THE DAY OF EVIL COMES, YOU MAY BE ABLE TO STAND YOUR GROUND, AND AFTER YOU HAVE DONE EVERYTHING, TO STAND. [14]STAND FIRM THEN, WITH THE BELT OF

TRUTH BUCKLED AROUND YOUR WAIST, WITH THE BREASTPLATE OF RIGHTEOUSNESS IN PLACE, [15]AND WITH YOUR FEET FITTED WITH THE READINESS THAT COMES FROM THE GOSPEL OF PEACE. [16]IN ADDITION TO ALL THIS, TAKE UP THE SHIELD OF FAITH, WITH WHICH YOU CAN EXTINGUISH ALL THE FLAMING ARROWS OF THE EVIL ONE. [17]TAKE THE HELMET OF SALVATION AND THE SWORD OF THE SPIRIT, WHICH IS THE WORD OF GOD."

EPHESIANS 6:10-17

The scriptures above offer guidance. To make sure I have all of my protection on, I start with my head and move down my body.

The first piece of armor is the Helmet of Salvation. We just talked about that. If you haven't turned your life over to Jesus, stop right here and do it. Your eternal life depends on putting that piece on!

The second piece of our armor is the breastplate of Righteousness. What does that mean? The definition of righteousness is the state of being righteous, characterized by acting in an upright and moral way, conforming to proper virtuous and ethical principles, being chaste and refraining from immorality. In short, it's to emulate Jesus and conduct ourselves as God would want us to. When I understood that I'm only righteous because of Jesus, I knew that I could put on that plate.

*"THIS **RIGHTEOUSNESS** IS GIVEN THROUGH FAITH IN JESUS CHRIST TO ALL WHO BELIEVE."*

ROMANS 3:22

The third piece of armor is the Belt of Truth.

"BUT IN YOUR HEARTS REVERE CHRIST AS LORD. ALWAYS BE PREPARED TO GIVE AN ANSWER TO EVERYONE WHO ASKS YOU TO GIVE THE REASON FOR THE HOPE THAT YOU HAVE. BUT DO THIS WITH GENTLENESS AND RESPECT."

1 PETER 3:15

Can I tell someone the truth? Yes, I want a heart of love, gentleness, and respect, seasoned with salt.

The fourth piece of armor is "feet prepared with the Gospel of Peace." We need to be able to walk the walk and talk the talk! The gospel of peace to me is to be able to have peace when negative or upsetting things in life happen.

Reread the following:

"FOR OUR STRUGGLE IS NOT AGAINST FLESH AND BLOOD, BUT AGAINST THE RULERS, AGAINST THE AUTHORITIES, AGAINST THE POWERS OF THIS DARK WORLD AND AGAINST THE SPIRITUAL FORCES OF EVIL IN THE HEAVENLY REALMS."

EPHESIANS 6:12

Understand that our struggle absolutely is against the powers of the dark world and the spiritual forces of evil. When you consider this and understand it, you'll realize that this throws wrenches into our plans. Thankfully, there's another piece of armor to help us keep our peace.

The fifth piece is the Shield of Faith. To reiterate, reread the following brief passage:

"IN ADDITION TO ALL THIS, TAKE UP THE SHIELD OF FAITH, WITH WHICH YOU CAN EXTINGUISH ALL THE FLAMING ARROWS OF THE EVIL ONE."

EPHESIANS 6:16B

This piece is the one that I struggled with the most. For a long time, I read the scriptures but didn't know they were true. Sure, I read them and believed that they were from God. Where I failed was that I didn't accept that they actually could be real and help me. My life changed when I got to the place where I had Faith that God didn't just put these words down for knowledge; He gave them to us as promises and for battle.

My faith in God was now real, not just a thought or idea. It was active and alive! That's why some call it the living word; I understand what that means now. Finally, there was the Sword of the Spirit, meaning the Word of God.

"FOR THE WORD OF GOD IS ALIVE AND ACTIVE. SHARPER THAN ANY DOUBLE-EDGED SWORD, IT PENETRATES EVEN TO DIVIDING SOUL AND SPIRIT, JOINTS AND MARROW; IT JUDGES THE THOUGHTS AND ATTITUDES OF THE HEART."

HEBREWS 4:12

When I started memorizing and quoting God's Word out loud – using my sword in an active way – my life was transformed. In your quiet time of prayer, when you're praying for protection over family members, yourself, and friends, believe that it's true, that there is a hedge of protection surrounding them so that nothing can get through and harm them. Believe it, not just say it, but pray it! **Gods Protection!**

Chapter 4

Purity

Scripture

*"Finally, brothers and sisters, whatever is true, whatever is noble, whatever is right, whatever is **pure**, whatever is lovely, whatever is admirable – if anything is excellent or praiseworthy – think about such things."*

Philippians 4:8

Dictionary

Purity is freedom from evil, adulteration or contamination.

I've been working hard on being pure in all that I do. I try to think before I act, react, or say something I might regret. While writing this, I felt the need to apologize to a friend about something I'd said about another friend. It was something I shouldn't have said.

I felt regret as soon as the words rolled off my tongue. Immediately after I said what could be classified as a gossip, I was convicted. I had a few options of what I could choose to do with my remorseful feelings and conviction. I could've said, "It wasn't that big of a deal," and minimized it. Another choice was to justify it as the truth. Choosing not to deal with it by sweeping it under the rug was another option. Within a few minutes of uttering those unfortunate words, I apologized to him for talking about my other friend.

Besides purity in how I think, it's also how I talk and act when no one is watching me. Some have called this integrity, and others refer to it as good character. I believe it's all the same thing. I classify it as being pure since purity is the avoidance of anything in our minds or hearts that's unclean. Had I not chosen to apologize to my friend for the words I know I shouldn't have said, I would be disappointed in myself for my failure to act in a pure way.

Where it concerns my relationship with the friend I had spoken out of place to, what would've been the consequences of my impure words? Maybe nothing. Then again, maybe he would've wondered, "Does he say things about me when I am not around?" I know what I said could easily be classified as gossip; I'm talking about global purity – to be pure in all things. I could've damaged my relationship with him. Is that what I want to be known as, a gossip, a man with no integrity? Absolutely not.

Now here's the big question: Am I a coward and too weak to face what I've done?

Not too many years ago, I wasn't strong enough to face the consequences of my actions, well, maybe it was a lot of years ago. I'm pretty old now, and over the years I've hit that conviction wall often. I come away with a bloody nose many times, figuratively speaking, of course.

As I've grown to understand, many people are happy to forgive if you have a heart willing to admit, "I screwed up!" Unfortunately, others aren't. You must be able to handle the ramifications of your actions to keep a pure heart, no matter how it's received. Humble yourself and ask for forgiveness when you've hurt someone or made a mistake. It's the right thing to do even though the person you apologize to may not be very receptive or nice to you. The poorly chosen actions are yours; you need to be able to take responsibility and accept the consequences. Although unthinkable for me, the following is a good example of varying consequences. If I would murder someone and then go forward and confessed, "I did it," the consequences would be much different than if I told a little white lie to someone or gossiped. Would you expect the ramifications to be the same? I don't think so!

In situations like these, it's righteous to ask God to help me make things right. When I do this, I get my peace back. It's good to have a pure conscience, both with the person or people I've sinned against and especially to God. I can tell you this from experience, whether I had screwed up big time or a little, my peace was restored.

"THEREFORE CONFESS YOUR SINS TO EACH OTHER AND PRAY FOR EACH OTHER SO THAT YOU MAY BE HEALED. THE PRAYER OF A RIGHTEOUS PERSON IS POWERFUL AND EFFECTIVE."

JAMES 5:16

I share my improprieties – my sins – with my friends. There's a difference between meekness and weakness. According to the dictionary, weakness is, "The state or condition of lacking strength." The definition of meekness is, "The fact or condition of being meek; submissiveness." A few synonyms of meekness are patience, long-suffering, forbearance, resignation, gentleness, mildness, softness, peacefulness, docility, modesty, humility, and list goes on and on. There's strength in meekness; a weak person would struggle with it. I'd certainly rather be meek than weak. Meek is Godly.

A friend of mine tells a story about a large football player he knows who spent years estranged from his brother. Their relationship was so bad it was nonexistent. I'm sure there are some of you reading this that have had major fallings out with family members, disagreements that have lasted for years. Undoubtedly you can understand the division and emotional distance, which my friend spoke about, between these two grown men.

My friend told me that recently there had been a family reunion planned, and both the brothers felt they should attend. They also knew they wouldn't be able to avoid each other completely while there. On the day of the gathering, the tension was great. The football player chose to go up to his brother meekly and allow him to chew him up one side and down the other. He stood there motionless with his hands behind his back while his brother raged, pointed his finger in his face, and used words purity prevents me from repeating.

After the brother vented his anger, and he had calmed down a little, the football player asked, "Are you done?"

"Yes, I am!" his brother grumbled.

That's when the football player grabbed his brother, gave him a big hug, and kissed him on the cheek. He said, "I love you, brother, and I'm sorry."

What could the brother who'd raged say then? Surely, he could've still held a grudge, but his football-playing brother had humbled himself and apologized. The sibling who'd raged realized his brother had done all he could to be the man that God wanted him to be. In turn, he chose to let go of his anger and resentment. It takes courage, not to let pride, fear, and the voices in your mind, to stop you from being pure and at peace.

My friend asked the football player why he chose to do what he did. All his friend said was, "I had to take the humble route."

Are you ready to be pure and meek and choose the humble route, too?

I know my perception of purity probably differs from the way some people see it. There are many different ways to view it. If you think about pure water, what comes to mind? It has no impurities in it at all – it's clear! When you think about a pure heart, what does that mean to you? It should be that there's nothing unclean in it.

Let's talk about the physical heart. If there are some impurities in it, what do you think happens? It gets sluggish, or worse; it stops working. It's the same way with your spiritual heart.

When you let enough stuff clog your spiritual heart, bad things start to develop. If you don't deal with the things that cause you to stumble, what happens then? Your peace is lost and you likely become jaded. You may justify your attitude by saying, "Everybody does it."

I have a friend of mine that told me a story about his father. His dad, a religious man, had some good friends over for supper. In the conversation, he asked, "Is it okay to watch R-rated movies?"

"Sure it is," replied one friend.

Another said, "It doesn't hurt anything."

His other friend added, "It's not a problem if you only watch it every once in a while."

Soon after that, the host approached that table with a pan of brownies that were fresh from the oven. It was obvious to his guest he was about to serve the fresh, hot dessert. They relished the tempting aroma as they waited anxiously for a piece.

"Those smell so good," one friend remarked. The other friends agreed in unison.

"I think you're going to enjoy them. I made them from scratch."

"I have no doubt," said one friend. "I love everything you cook; this won't be any different."

Another of the guest said, "They smell incredible; what do you have in them?"

"Oh," my friend's father said, "butter, sugar, flour, eggs, cocoa powder, a little honey, and a pinch of poop from my poodle."

His friends gasped, "What? That's terrible! How gross!"

Do you think that his friends ate those brownies? There's not a chance of it. They instantly perceived them as tainted, something they wouldn't think of putting into their mouths. The level of impurity made no difference to them. They recognized that the brownies were unclean and contaminated.

Now I am not condemning or judging you for watching R rated movies. I'm just trying to make a point about purity. There are so many movies I'd like to see that I choose to avoid because I can't allow those little impurities in my life. It doesn't take much to contaminate our souls. A little here and a little there all adds up. My point with the poodle poop story was to help you understand that even a little bit of impurity affects you. Now that I've realized this, the Holy Spirit has moved me to make a personal decision. I choose not to watch R-rated movies."

That is my choice – I'm aware I can't be your Holy Spirit. What I can do is share what I do to stay pure, to plant a seed, if you will.

Purity is a journey; it's one we take one step at a time. I, like you, strive to improve my relationship with God. My decision to avoid R-rated movies is only the tip of the mountain that I've climbed in my journey. While I still have a long way to go, I feel that I'm moving to the higher ground of purity. That pleases me and I know my efforts also please God.

It's a daily walk. It is not something I believe I can conquer on my own. In fact, I know I can't do it by myself. If I wouldn't have constant communication with something greater than me, and also my like-minded friends around me, who encourage me and help me to be better, I'd be lost and miserable. I implore you to do your best to travel the higher road and always to be green and growing, instead of red and rotten.

I challenge you to pray for a pure heart and mind for someone close to you. Ask those nearest to you to pray for you also, and then watch what happens in your lives. Your walk with God will be so much better. Everyone around will have their walk with Him improve, too. A pure heart and a pure mind will help you and the people you pray for have a fruitful life of significance!

Strive for Purity!

Chapter 5

Peace

Scripture

6 "Do not be anxious about anything, but in every situation, by prayer and petition, with thanksgiving, present your requests to God. 7And the peace of God, which transcends all understanding, will guard your hearts and your minds in Christ Jesus."

Philippians 4:6-7

Dictionary

Peace is a stress-free state of security and calmness that comes when there's no fighting or war; when everything coexists in perfect harmony and freedom.

When I am not in control, I sometimes feel anxious about it. I choose to look to the Bible for encouragement.

"The Lord will fight for you; you need only to be still."

Exodus 14:14

"Do not be anxious about anything."

Philippians 4:6

Does that mean I have to give up control? That's exactly what it means! Because I believe the scriptures and trust in the Lord, I **can** give up control.

As I've grown in this area, I find that I'm able to get my peace back in an instant. It took me some time, practice, and some difficult situations to know that God has my back.

26 "Look at the birds of the air; they do not sow or reap or store away in barns, and yet your heavenly Father feeds them. Are you not much more valuable than they? 27Can any one of you by worrying add a single hour to your life?"
28 "And why do you worry about clothes? See how the flowers of the

FIELD GROW. THEY DO NOT LABOR OR SPIN.
[29]YET I TELL YOU THAT NOT EVEN SOLOMON
IN ALL HIS SPLENDOR WAS DRESSED LIKE
ONE OF THESE. [30]IF THAT IS HOW GOD
CLOTHES THE GRASS OF THE FIELD, WHICH
IS HERE TODAY AND TOMORROW IS THROWN
INTO THE FIRE, WILL HE NOT MUCH MORE
CLOTHE YOU—YOU OF LITTLE FAITH? [31]SO
DO NOT WORRY, SAYING, 'WHAT SHALL
WE EAT?' OR 'WHAT SHALL WE DRINK?'
OR 'WHAT SHALL WE WEAR?' [32]FOR THE
PAGANS RUN AFTER ALL THESE THINGS,
AND YOUR HEAVENLY FATHER KNOWS THAT
YOU NEED THEM. [33]BUT SEEK FIRST HIS
KINGDOM AND HIS RIGHTEOUSNESS, AND
ALL THESE THINGS WILL BE GIVEN TO YOU
AS WELL. [34]THEREFORE DO NOT WORRY
ABOUT TOMORROW, FOR TOMORROW WILL
WORRY ABOUT ITSELF. EACH DAY HAS
ENOUGH TROUBLE OF ITS OWN."

MATTHEW 6:26-34

The turning point for me was when I realized that I don't have control over my life. I'm not a man of little faith; I've learned from the teachings of Matthew, above, and I no longer worry about what I'll wear or what I'll eat.

When my faith in God grew, so did my peace. Now when I realize I am anxious, I examine my situation. Am I letting the things of this world control me to make me feel this way? Do I doubt that God, the creator of the earth and universe, can help me? Do I have so much faith in my abilities that I believe I can take whatever is going on and fix it better than God can? I've found over the years that I'm weak in a lot of ways, but I'm reassured that I can trust in our all-powerful God. When I find myself anxious, I choose not to hold onto it. I rely upon scriptures to get rid of it quickly. I recite them to release the grip of whatever it is that's trying to trip me up. The difference is that I no longer avoid situations that involve abilities I doubt I possess. I proceed forward with whatever I need to say or do, confident that God will provide.

I ask God to give me the strength and wisdom to handle the circumstances in advance. For instance, if there is something awkward I need to deal with, or if I need to confront someone involved in a situation that may have hurt me or someone I love or care about, I turn to God.

> *"IF ANY OF YOU LACKS WISDOM, YOU SHOULD ASK GOD, WHO GIVES GENEROUSLY TO ALL WITHOUT FINDING FAULT, AND IT WILL BE GIVEN TO YOU."*
>
> *JAMES 1:5*

I also must stand on verses 6-8:

6"*BUT WHEN YOU ASK, YOU MUST BELIEVE AND NOT DOUBT, BECAUSE THE ONE WHO DOUBTS IS LIKE A WAVE OF THE SEA, BLOWN AND TOSSED BY THE WIND. 7THAT PERSON SHOULD NOT EXPECT TO RECEIVE ANYTHING FROM THE LORD. 8SUCH A PERSON IS DOUBLE-MINDED AND UNSTABLE IN ALL THEY DO.*"

JAMES 1:6-8

I'll be the first to admit that those verses are kind of scary! I push through the uncomfortable feelings and understand that God handles all situations if I let Him.

I'm human, and to be honest, sometimes I still doubt. Even through my failings, I ask Him for His favor and move forward. I have to remember not to let fear or doubt stop me from a confrontation that needs to happen. Over time, through prayer and outright asking God for wisdom, He has allowed me to have victories and successes. Through His grace, they both became far greater than the failures, and I began to find my peace.

Not that long ago, or so it feels, I was a twenty-three-year-old young man who was born again. Since then – and I'm writing this at the tender age of fifty-eight – I've tried to navigate through life as a Christian. It's been important to me that I not step on anyone's toes or hurt their feelings, yet I was still stressed. I had a hard time keeping my peace, and I didn't know why. I knew I was saved and forgiven for my sins, but I would still lose my peace often and not know how to get it back.

Finally, I realized I could control myself with God's direction and guidance, and my peace would stay with me longer. I also understood that I had no control over anyone else's feelings or emotions, although I could help them navigate through their troubled waters. Over the years, I've found I like assisting people who needed to talk to someone. Smart enough not to be a know-it-all, coupled with God-given gifts of being both a good listener and willing to share my personal trials and tribulations, I've found this to be one of my callings. I've overcome some pretty ugly things in my life, and I've learned from those experiences. Time and time again, it's proven to disarm and to comfort people when I freely share my low points. Their confidence is safe with me, and I believe most people can sense that. It gives them the freedom to share their "stuff" and feel safe, not judged.

I have a church friend, who for many years, decades actually, was little more than an acquaintance to me. He was a well-respected pillar of my church and community. While I think of myself as someone who's an open book, up until that point, this man and I had only made small talk about the weather and our children.

One day we met for lunch. He and I shook hands and shared our "It's good-to-see-ya" pleasantries. We had known each other for over twenty-five years by this time. I'd watched his kids grow up, saw what he had done for the church, and noticed his success, yet our friendship was still rather superficial.

That changed that day when he said, "Let me give you some history about me." As I sat and listened, he told me about his life and how certain events shaped him into the man he had grown to be. I was honored that he let me see the real man, not the one I'd known from a distance, the one I thought I knew.

You're probably wondering, "What in the world does that have to do with peace?" It has a lot to do with my peace, and it's an example for you where it concerns yours. This man was well-known and looked up to in the community.

He was someone I admired, but he was also someone I was guarded around, even somewhat intimidated by, I'm sad to say. I was worried that my story would be a shock to him, and he wouldn't like the person that I really am. Thankfully, I seriously underestimated him. His candor with me put me at ease, and the openness and honesty of his words comforted me. You see, I sat down at the table that day feeling apprehensive about a one-on-one visit with him. This was no twenty second visit, nor did I have others around me to share in his attention; this was he and I alone for lunch and a good chat. Intently I listened as he shared his story. He was receptive to hear about my life, too, a story I found myself sharing with him with ease. Through our candid conversation, our friendship grew closer than I could've imagined. My peace, which I admit had been disrupted when we first sat down together, was now intact.

Thinking back on that encounter, I'm reminded that ALL people have issues that they have gone through, or are going through. I'm not alone with my issues, and neither are you. God carries us all, and He wants us to come to Him and REST in Him. That's where my peace is, and where it always will be – in God!

The next time you visit with a Christian brother or sister that you don't know well, be open, honest, and vulnerable with them. Let God show you how great He is! Exposing who you truly are is scary at first, but it gets easier as you do it more.

When you're able to be honest and open with more people, you'll see and build relationships that'll last a lifetime. When you're honest, loving, and giving, and you believe there's good in all, your peace and joy will increase. Contemplate the possibilities with the people that are in your life, but not especially close to you. I hope you build greater and deeper relationships, more and better than you thought you could. It'll enrich your life as well as theirs.

Pray for peace for someone that you feel truly needs it. Surely you know at least one unsettled person that could use the gift of peace. It's the right thing to do, and by doing His work and praying for peace for someone else, you'll see how God will reveal His **peace** to you!

Chapter 6

Prosperity

Scripture

"In his days may the righteous flourish and prosperity abound till the moon is no more."

Psalm 72:7

Dictionary

Prosperity is the state of being prosperous; advance or gain in anything good or desirable; successful progress in any business or enterprise; attainment of the object desired; good fortune; success; as, commercial prosperity; national prosperity.

Is prosperity just a financial concept? Can you be prosperous in your family? Can you be prosperous in your relationships? I'm asking these questions because most of the time we relate prosperity to money or success.

In order to raise good members of society, we direct our children to do right and make good choices. Can that be classified as prosperity? What about if you help build up a friend, family member, or a brother or sister in Christ to become a better person? Could you encourage them to excel at what they do, or motivate them to have a better relationship with their family or spouse? I believe these are prime examples of being prosperous.

I want to examine prosperity in a way that we see the whole picture, not just the pieces. Let's look at what prosperity is and what it isn't. I'm going to get into some things that might cause you to think, "I've felt that before" or "I've done that before." So, let's get to it.

By the time I was eight years old, my family had moved seven times to seven different cities in four states. I know what you are thinking, "He was a military brat." Nope, I'm the son of a man that struggled with gambling, women, and alcohol. Later I learned that we moved to escape harm after my dad repeatedly fell deeply into debt with locals. This had taken place in the 1960s, long before you could use the Internet to find someone who had skipped town. I know many of my younger readers can't truly relate to what life was like before social media and the internet; suffice it to say that it was harder to find a person than it is now. My family moved a lot.

On the outside, we looked like a successful family. We had nice houses and fine cars. My dad was a salesman. He could have been the president of the United States, and I believe that with all my heart. He was smart, good-looking, and charismatic, but he was lost. He was always searching for that next win and loading his empty bucket of a heart and soul with things that didn't fulfill him.

On the outside, we looked to be a good, prosperous family. We were the family everybody wanted to be like, or so it appeared. There was a time when we were hobnobbing with TV stars and big business people. We belonged to various country clubs, and my dad golfed with executives of big companies.

In the eyes of man, we were prosperous and successful. As you already know, that wasn't our reality. Perhaps it's not yours. The secrets, the lies, the pain!

I've learned that prosperity is when I can get up in the morning from a great night's sleep, in a safe home, with my bills paid, and the peace of knowing that I have someone looking over me that controls the entire universe. I hope that makes sense to you because as you've read, I didn't have that during the first eight years of my life.

Actually, I didn't have it at all while growing up. I was lost and didn't know where or what prosperity truly meant until I was in my fifties.

Please keep reading as I share more of my background and past. My walk has been a challenging one; I desire to encourage you by sharing my story. Awareness is 98% of the cure because it helps when you believe there's hope. By being open about my trials and tribulations, I hope to help you find fruitful prosperity quicker than I did.

I have to commend my grandparents for taking their daughter back in, along with her eight year old and nine month old children. Remember, too, that this was in a time where divorce wasn't nearly as readily accepted. Still, they did what they knew would be best for us. My mom left my dad to get away from the craziness and fear – and to raise my sister and me in a normal, stable environment in a small town in Louisiana.

Back there, my grandparents were part of the local Baptist church congregation. My grandfather was a pipefitter and a member of the pipefitter's union. He and my grandma were well-known in town and solid in the community. They were liked and stable.

I didn't know what my life was going to be like, but after moving around so much, I did know how to acclimate to new schools and make new friends. I just went where I was told to go and adapted to my surroundings.

Did I understand what prosperity was at eight years old? No, I didn't. Was I aware of what was truly happening to my family and me? Nope. Did I know the difference between the life I had with my dad versus what my life was going to be like living with my mom, sister, and grandparents? No, not really. To sum it up, I had no clue what was going on, and I didn't know how it was going to affect me in my journey through life – but affect me, it did. I didn't understand what prosperity was, nor did I have a clue if we had it or not. Now, I know that we most decidedly did **not** have it.

My mom was a homemaker; I don't remember her working out of the house before this time. We had nothing. Mom moved us into a small rent house right on the highway where big eighteen-wheelers would pass at all hours. One night when I was ten or eleven years old, she heard unsettling noises outside. Determined to protect us from whatever was out there, she grabbed a knife and closed us up together in our room. I can still see her leaning on the door with the knife, scared to death. I later realized she did all she knew how to do to protect us.

We all get caught up in our circumstances, be it our past or things that are happening to us at the moment. Often we go through life as if we have blinders on and we don't realize what's happening to us or around us. It's understandable, but there's a better way.

Eventually, I realized I wasn't that eight-year-old boy anymore. Neither was I that teenager who lacked guidance and good examples. When I became consciously aware of these facts, I was able to move forward. I no longer allowed my past to dictate who I am. I began to realize I had to live in the moment. God had *and* has a purpose for my life, and I should live one day and one moment at a time.

When negative circumstances arise, I turn to something greater than myself and know deep in my heart that I'm protected, provided for, and loved, no matter how I feel. My bucket is full, and when I look at someone in need, I can give of myself and help them. To me, being able to point them in the direction of peace, love, and forgiveness is true **prosperity!**

Chapter 7

Blessings

Scripture

[24]"The Lord bless you and keep you; [25]the Lord make his face shine on you and be gracious to you; [26]the Lord turn his face toward you and give you peace."

Numbers 6:24-26

Dictionary

The act or words of a person who blesses; a special favor, mercy, or benefit; a favor or gift bestowed by God, thereby bringing happiness; the invoking of God's favor upon a person.

I expect you're familiar with the saying, "Count your blessings one by one and really see what God has done." If you are or aren't, it's a good thing to remember. Try to think of this at least once a week and do it. If you haven't done it recently, stop right now and count your blessings. Go ahead; I'll wait…

If you're having a tough time thinking about how much you're blessed, it might help you to know some simple worldwide statistics. The World Health Organization and UNICEF report that 780,000,000 people don't have access to an improved water source. Think about that; we're talking about simple, clean water, something you probably take for granted. An estimated 2,500,000,000 people lack access to improved sanitation. That's more than 35% of the world's population. According to the United States Department of Housing and Urban Development's Annual Homeless Assessment Report, as of 2017, there were around 554,000 homeless people in the United States on any given night.

Now let us take a look at what most of us have. First, you likely have a roof over your head. No matter if you own or are renting your home, do you have a car in the driveway or parking lot?

There are about one billion cars in the world. However, there are seven-and-a-half billion people in the world. That means about six-and-a-half billion people aren't fortunate enough to have a car. Okay?

I could keep going, but I think you understand what I mean. I haven't pointed this out to make you feel guilty about having things; God wants us to prosper.

> *"IN HIS DAYS MAY THE RIGHTEOUS FLOURISH AND PROSPERITY ABOUND TILL THE MOON IS NO MORE."*
>
> *PSALM 72:7*

Without intending to step on anyone's toes, I want to point out that we should appreciate what we take for granted and stop concerning ourselves with those possessions we lack. We should look at what we do have.

It dawned on me that I should do this one evening while I was sitting on the edge of my bed. I was struggling financially and feeling down. Emotionally spent, I didn't know what to do. Then it hit me, and I started to look at what I had.

There I sat in a climate-controlled home, able to sleep in a warm, safe bed. I could go to the sink and get a glass of clean water. Although money was tight, I still had a little in my pocket. I have a wife that I feel loves me more than anyone else except God! Guys and gals, I fell off the bed and got on my knees and started thanking God for what I did have and where he had me.

I realize it's possible you're not in a good place right now. Please don't think I'm minimizing your difficulties or your struggles. I hope to aid you by sharing what helped me when I was low emotionally, spiritually, and desperate. Counting my blessings changed my heart and my thinking.

This might be a simple thing to some of you, but for me, it was life-changing. I had forgotten how blessed I was. Now I do everything I can to stay in the present and think about what I have, just in material things, much less my health and mind. No longer do I let the enemy blind me from the truth. It's not that I don't struggle and fail every once in a while; it's that it doesn't happen as often since I had this revelation.

I want to share with you the Beatitudes. In Matthew 5:1-2, he introduces us to the Sermon on the Mount that Jesus gave to his apostles early in his ministry. Jesus did this soon after he was baptized by John the Baptist. "Beatitudes" is derived from the Latin word beatus, which means blessed. In 5:3-10, Matthew recounts the eight blessings given to us by Jesus.

[1] *"NOW WHEN JESUS SAW THE CROWDS, HE WENT UP ON A MOUNTAINSIDE AND SAT DOWN. HIS DISCIPLES CAME TO HIM,* [2] *AND HE BEGAN TO TEACH THEM."*

[3] *"HE SAID: 'BLESSED ARE THE POOR IN SPIRIT, FOR THEIRS IS THE KINGDOM OF HEAVEN.*

[4] *BLESSED ARE THOSE WHO MOURN, FOR THEY WILL BE COMFORTED.*

[5] *BLESSED ARE THE MEEK, FOR THEY WILL INHERIT THE EARTH.*

[6] *BLESSED ARE THOSE WHO HUNGER AND THIRST FOR RIGHTEOUSNESS, FOR THEY WILL BE FILLED.*

[7] *BLESSED ARE THE MERCIFUL, FOR THEY WILL BE SHOWN MERCY.*

[8] *BLESSED ARE THE PURE IN HEART, FOR THEY WILL SEE GOD.*

[9] *BLESSED ARE THE PEACEMAKERS, FOR THEY WILL BE CALLED CHILDREN OF GOD.*

[10] *BLESSED ARE THOSE WHO ARE PERSECUTED BECAUSE OF RIGHTEOUSNESS, FOR THEIRS IS THE KINGDOM OF HEAVEN.*

[11] *BLESSED ARE YOU WHEN PEOPLE INSULT YOU, PERSECUTE YOU AND FALSELY SAY ALL*

KINDS OF EVIL AGAINST YOU BECAUSE OF ME.
[12] REJOICE AND BE GLAD, BECAUSE GREAT IS YOUR REWARD IN HEAVEN, FOR IN THE SAME WAY THEY PERSECUTED THE PROPHETS WHO WERE BEFORE YOU.'"

MATTHEW 5:1-12

When I studied the Beatitudes in Matthew, I got a little bummed, and uplifted, too. I had an idea of what being blessed meant in God's eyes, and also the things that I needed to work towards to make me a better man. I didn't have any guidance when I was younger, nor did I have good examples to follow, other than my grandparents. Unfortunately, we were only with them a few short years. As I got older, I started learning the Word and seeing men that were great examples of what was talked about in the scriptures. Both helped me gain a deeper understanding of what the Beatitudes meant.

The bottom line for me is that I want to be the best man I can be for my family, for my community, and most of all, for my God! It's not about what I do – it's what God and Jesus Christ have done for me.

At the risk of sounding too preachy, I want you to understand how adrift I was before Jesus came into my life. I was not only lost in my salvation, but in my life in general.

Now I have a rule book – I live by the teachings of the Holy Bible. It guides me, and it has helped me get to where I am today. I understand how blessed I am, not just monetarily, but also emotionally, spiritually, and physically.

Not all that long before the Lord took my grandmother home, she and I had a good conversation about spirituality. I asked her, "If you were to find out that there's no heaven, this late in life, would you change anything about how you lived yours?"

She said, "I'd live my life for Jesus, the same way I've done all along."

What a testament to her relationship with God – wow – she wouldn't have changed anything. How can I not follow her example? I'm truly **blessed!**

Chapter 8

Favor

Scripture

"Surely, Lord, you bless the righteous; you surround them with your favor as with a shield."

Psalm 5:12

Dictionary

Approval, support, or liking for someone or something. An act of kindness beyond what is due or usual.

When you think of favor, what comes to your mind? Are you asking for a favor or is someone asking you for one?

When I first heard someone say that they wanted God to show them favor, it was a foreign concept to me. What did that mean? Upon researching it, I found that **favor** is when God gives us a little lagniappe – a commonly used Cajun word that means "a little something extra." Look at it as an added blessing. I do not doubt He protects us from some things that we don't even know would happen. Have you ever been guided to a position or a situation you didn't expect, but had it work out surprisingly well for you? He looks out for us in little things, and big ones, too.

A small example is when I have to go to the mall at Christmas time. I try to avoid trips there, especially at such a busy time of the year for the stores. Like most people, I hope for a parking spot close to the entrance. I'll see it in my mind and believe that it's there. Most of the time it is, someone is backing out of a space, and it's available to me. I always remember to thank God for the favor on my life.

There are times when it doesn't happen, and I have to park much farther away than I wanted.

My faith in God leads me to believe He still has shown me his favor, even when what I hoped for wasn't provided. He could have had me park away from where I wanted for a safety reason. It might also be that He wants me to get some exercise. When I do have to park far away, I don't get frustrated. Instead, I thank God for looking out for me and my health.

It's probable that when you pray for favor over someone, you won't get to see the results of His actions for them, just as they won't see you blessing them with your prayers. When you pray for them, you get out of yourself and focus on someone else. God will show His favor on you for this, I can promise you.

Do you believe you have God's favor or are you one of those people that say, "God is so busy. How can he show me His favor?"

First, if you've turned your life over to Jesus, you already have his favor. Your faith is a gift from God!

> *"FOR IT IS BY GRACE YOU HAVE BEEN SAVED, THROUGH FAITH — AND THIS IS NOT FROM YOURSELVES, IT IS THE GIFT OF GOD."*
> *EPHESIANS 2:8*

When someone gives you a gift, do you respond with a reply such as, "You shouldn't have," and refuse it? No, you usually take it. We all know that it's rude not to accept a gift because the presenter has sacrificed something to give it to you. It could be money, an item they made or bought for you. They also had to take time out of their life to get the gift. No matter what it is, as long as it was given with a pure heart, there are no strings attached. That's how it is with the gift of favor from God. We've done nothing to receive it, yet we should accept it and thank Him for his favor. Are we aware of the gift of favor that God shines on us every day? No, we aren't. We should be thankful for His favor, both when we're aware of it and when we aren't.

My brother-in-law and other family members planned to go on a mission trip to Honduras one spring. During a gathering the Christmas before, I asked for the specific time and date they were to leave and when they expected to get to Honduras.

On that day, a group of us prayed for them throughout their travels. One of the prayers I prayed was for God to show favor to them as they traveled.

After their return, our family gathered for a crawfish boil. If you're not familiar with a crawfish boil, let me tell you it's a fun occasion with good friends, family, conversation, and food. After the event, my brother-in-law pulled my wife and me aside. He said he had a wild story to share with us.

It turns out he wanted to chronicle the strange turn of events that had happened on the day his group of fifteen headed to Honduras. My brother-in-law had left his home in Alexandria, Louisiana, early enough to drive the two hours to meet up with the rest of the group. The rendezvous was planned for 5:30 a.m. at the airport in Shreveport. Upon arrival, they found that their connecting flight to Houston, Texas had been canceled.

With no viable flight options available to get them to Houston in time, they prayed about it and decided to make the three-and-a-half to four hour drive. Time was of the essence because their flight to San Pedro Sula, Honduras was to take off at 9:35 a.m., now less than four hours away.

They were granted God's favor for their trip to Houston. They arrived safely at 9:05 a.m. when their flight was to start boarding.

The first four attendants they spoke with told them they couldn't make their flight. There was just too much that needed to happen before the plane backed away from the gate. They needed boarding passes, and they still had to go through TSA.

One of the men in the group got a text from the airline. He showed my brother-in-law, who promptly showed it to the attendant who had been delivering the bad news. They were holding the plane for them!

She said they should unload their luggage while she spoke to her supervisors. Ten minutes later, two supervisors showed up and saw to it that they were processed through. The airline was indeed holding the plane loaded with roughly two hundred people for my brother-in-law's group.

There was a lot of luggage because each of the fifteen of them had two fifty-pound bags of supplies and a personal carry-on bag. The attendants made sure all of the luggage was loaded. The TSA even created a special line for them. And if that wasn't enough, two members of their team were given first-class seats because there wasn't enough room left in the economy section for all of them.

In the end, the plane was delayed for a little over an hour to make sure they'd get to Honduras that day. Because of that, they had the opportunity to build a house for three ladies and teach one hundred eight children Vacation Bible School in a Honduran public school. If you believe that's God's favor, as I do, shout a loud AMEN!

My brother-in-law choked up while recounting the events to us because he knew we had been praying for him and his team. It was a gift to us that he told us at the crawfish boil because had he not, we would never have known our prayers had been answered.

It's a gift when we're made aware our prayers were answered; most of the time we'll never know. Still, we should pray for favor over someone because we never know what God is going to do for them.

Kenny, a brother in Christ of mine, when asked how he's doing, routinely says, "I'm highly favored and blessed." You should know you are, too. When you pray for favor over someone, remember that and pass it on to the people you love and those that come to your heart and mind.

Right now, I want you to think of someone and pray this over them. "Lord, please show your favor over – <u>you fill in the blank</u> – and guide them in your love and Grace." I know that no matter how I feel, that always picks me up and fills my heart. Do this in your study time and throughout the day. You'll see a transformation both in your life and the lives you pray **favor** over.

Chapter 9

Overflow

Scripture

[5]"You prepare a table before me in the presence of my enemies. You anoint my head with oil; my cup overflows. [6]Surely your goodness and love will follow me all the days of my life, and I will dwell in the house of the Lord forever."

Psalm 23:5-6

Dictionary

To flow over the brim of, to flow over bounds, to fill a space to capacity and spread beyond its limits.

Whenen I go into a convenience store to get my favorite beverage at the fountain drink machine, I tend to fill it to the top. The problem is that on occasion it overflows onto my hand and I even have to sip some out to get the lid on. Don't judge me! I know you've done this, too.

Now that I am thirsty, I'll get to my point. You see, the cup can only contain so much fluid. When we try to put too much in it, some of it must go somewhere else. When God fills us to overflow with His blessings, His prosperity, and His favor, it must go somewhere.

Where do you think your overflowing of His blessings goes? Hopefully, it blesses the people around you. We have to make some choices when it comes to overflow in our life. We can choose to not do anything with it, or we may feel we need to keep it for ourselves because we might need it later. Or we can trust that God has given us this overflow for a reason and that it's to bless others.

Surely you've heard someone say, "If I won the lottery, I'd help my kids and my family." That overflow is financial. Overflow means so much more than that to me. When I pray for overflow for someone, I believe that God will shower them with more than they can think or imagine.

> *"Now to him who is able to do immeasurably more than all we ask or imagine, according to his power that is at work within us."*
>
> *Ephesians 3:20*

True overflow isn't limited to financial rewards. It's in all aspects of our lives: health, wealth, and a peaceful, productive life.

On an episode of one of my favorite television shows one of the main characters compared his life to someone he viewed as rich. The other man had abundant money, but he also had turmoil in his life because of it. I'm not saying that money is bad; be cautious of the attitude that often comes with it.

The main character said he was happy with his life. He had a job he loved, friends he cared for, and friends who cared about him. These brought him joy, and they were things that money couldn't buy. He had true contentment. He was able to share his overflow with the person he was talking to, one that struggled to understand how he didn't long to have as much money as the rich guy. He was pleased with his life and wary of the pain that often comes with an excess of money.

When we're overflowing, we have everything we need, plus more of what we want. We can and should bless others, not just think of ourselves. What does overflowing look like to you? Think about it deeply – do a heart check – and decide what contentment means to you. What's enough for you?

"Enough" is different for all of us. You and God need to have a heart-to-heart about where He wants you and where you want to be. Do this so that you can pray for overflow, and then, in turn, give from your overflow as God blesses you. Remember to give from your heart and not just from your abundance.

Overflow is one of the greatest words you can pray over someone. God promises to take care of all of the desires of our hearts; overflow is beyond our needs and desires.

> *"TAKE DELIGHT IN THE LORD, AND HE WILL GIVE YOU THE DESIRES OF YOUR HEART."*
>
> PSALM 37:4

I'll go even further – God already knows your wants and needs. He knows every hair on your head.

> *"INDEED, THE VERY HAIRS OF YOUR HEAD ARE ALL NUMBERED. DON'T BE AFRAID; YOU ARE WORTH MORE THAN MANY SPARROWS."*
> *LUKE 12:7*

I do not doubt that the God of all creation wants to shower you with overflow. As a father and grandfather, I want to give to my kids and grandkids. I love them, and He loves us all, including you.

Don't assume I'm speaking of financial gifts alone. I want to help my loved ones grow, to nurture them, and help them make good, sound decisions in life. Their spiritual life is important to me. Have they turned their lives over to Jesus? If not, what's holding them back? Do I share with them the details of my life before I was saved? Is my relationship with them one where I can be truthful with them out of love?

I'm not talking about young children; I'm referring to the older ones that haven't been born again. Our little ones need us to be examples for them, too, because we might be the only Jesus they see.

I hope you've been in a bible-believing church and that your kids have been prayed for before they were even born. They will know the love of the Lord from the example you are to them. Those of us who had a late start in life with our walk with Jesus are much less sure of how to share our love of God with our loved ones. That's okay, at the least we have that relationship with Him now, and He will guide us.

I believe that when our little ones are old enough to understand right from wrong, it's time we should talk with them about having a strong relationship with God of their own.

If nothing else, you've planted a seed, one that you and God can nurture and help grow in them. I'm aware that when my kids turned their lives over to Jesus, it may not have been due to my words, but instead a result of my prayers. I prayed for them and asked God to send people into their lives that would be bold enough to share the Bible with them and help them navigate through it. As you know, most kids go through a stage where they believe their parents don't know anything. We must stand our ground and be that example that Jesus wants us to be.

"START CHILDREN OFF ON THE WAY THEY SHOULD GO, AND EVEN WHEN THEY ARE OLD THEY WILL NOT TURN FROM IT."

PROVERBS 22:6

That is my overflow. Not only am I going to see Jesus, but my kids will also! How about *that* for overflow? It brings peace to me to know their blinders are off and their place in Heaven is written in the book of life.

*"ANYONE WHOSE NAME WAS **NOT** FOUND WRITTEN IN THE BOOK OF LIFE HE WAS THROWN INTO THE LAKE OF FIRE."*

REVELATION 20:15

The Book of Life, in this context, is the set of names of those who will live with God forever in heaven. It's the role of those who have been saved. Now that the ones you've prayed for are saved, too, what can you do to help them? As mature Christians, we can make sure they have the tools they need to thrive in their walk with Jesus on this earth.

What does this mean? If you've been a Christian for any length of time you know there's more of your journey ahead as you walk through the lost world around you.

"BUT SMALL IS THE GATE AND NARROW THE ROAD THAT LEADS TO LIFE."

MATTHEW 7:14

There's always a battle to fight. How are we going to handle that fight when it is at our home or with our kids?

Whether in overflow or not, God is our Father through the saving grace of Jesus Christ. Why wouldn't He shower us with overflow? Are we so self-absorbed that we only think of ourselves and what other people can do for us?

When I was young, my cup was empty. How could I give to others as I struggled to fill my cup? Many of God's children find themselves in the same place. Do you battle with an addiction of some kind? Are you watching things on the Internet that you know you shouldn't be viewing? Do you try to buy the pain away? What's your internal conflict?

The only true way, the healthy way to fill your cup and take care of your pain and emptiness is to seek out the love and grace of Jesus Christ. Accept His gift and allow His love and blessings to overflow in you. Then you can help others fill their cups in return.

It's my sincere hope that I've helped you understand what overflow means to me. It's not simply words; it's action as it relates to the blessings I've received. When I pray for overflow, I believe the person I'm praying for will receive this gift from God. I also pray that they'll be filled with overflow and use their gifts from God to pass it on and bless the next person with it. Pray for **overflow**!

Reflection

I have a prayer for all who have read my book.

May God give you **Wisdom** to conquer your fears and doubts. May He give you **Purpose** to succeed in all that He puts in your path. May He **Protect** you from the evil one so you can be safe and secure in your walk with Him. Lord, please give them a **Pure** heart, one that is totally honest with you and the people they love. May your **Peace** surpass all understanding and be upon them throughout their life. Shower your **Prosperity** onto them so that they can share it with others. **Bless** them, Oh Lord, with the blessings that can only come from You. May your **Favor** be upon them so that they will see Your love and be able to share it with others. Shower them with **Overflow** to the max, so that they will be able to bless their family and others that You put in their heart!

I love you with all of my heart, Jeffrey.

Footnotes

Amy Peterson wrote, "To seek wisdom is ultimately to seek God, the source of all wisdom and understanding. And the wisdom that comes from above is worth more than any treasure we could ever imagine."

†Amy Peterson, *Our Daily Bread*®, © 2018 by Our Daily Bread Ministries, Grand Rapids, MI. Reprinted by permission. All rights reserved. March 2, 2018

Elisa Morgan wrote, "God stitches His love and purposes in our hearts that we might experience Him for ourselves and demonstrate His handiwork to others."

††Elisa Morgan, *Our Daily Bread*®, © 2018 by Our Daily Bread Ministries, Grand Rapids, MI. Reprinted by permission. All rights reserved. March 21, 2018

Announcements

Dear readers,

As this book goes to press, it's my intention to expand upon each of these words in follow-up books. To stay informed as those develop, follow me on my website at http://www.afruitfullife.net or my Facebook page: https://www.facebook.com/afruitfulLifeofSignificance.

The links above are also where you'll find dates and information for my upcoming book signings. I hope to see you at one of these engagements. I sincerely expect to enjoy talking to you.

A Fruitful Life of Significance is available in paperback ordered from Amazon, Barnes & Noble, Books-A-Million, Angus & Roberts, and other retailers.

The electronic eBook is available on Amazon for Kindles, or to be read for free with your Kindle Unlimited subscription.

If you'd like a personalized and signed copy of *A Fruitful Life of Significance,* they're available directly from me. Please contact me at Jeffrey@afruitfullife.net.

I'd love to share the word by speaking with your group, organization, or church. Email me at Jeffrey@afrutfullife.net, and we'll set something up.

Thank you, and my God bless you all the days of your life.

Jeffrey